RICHARD DANIELPOUR

T0066113

THREE MEZZO-SOPRANO ARIAS

FROM MARGARET GARNER

VOICE AND PIANO

text by Toni Morrison

Margaret's Lullaby

A Quality Love

Intermezzo

AMP 8218

First Printing: January 2007

ISBN-13: 978-1-4234-1661-6

ISBN-10: 1-4234-1661-9

Associated Music Publishers, Inc.

DISTRIBUTED BY

HAL•LEONARD®
CORPORATION

7777 W. BLUEMOUND RD. P.O. BOX 13819 MILWAUKEE, WI 53213

"Margaret Garner" was commissioned by the Michigan Opera Theatre, Cincinnati Opera Association and The Opera Company of Philadelphia.

When all three arias are sung together, the title "Triptych from Margaret Garner" may be used, and in this form it was commissioned by the Wheeling Symphony for a world premiere on 19 May 2006.

duration 16'

Triptych features Margaret Garner's understanding of love. These are Margaret's three feature arias in the opera, but each one shows her character's love in different ways. The first aria ["Margaret's Lullaby"] is a mother's love for her children. The second ["A Quality Love"] is an understanding of herself as a person to be loved. The final movement ["Intermezzo and Soliloquy"] shows Margaret speak about love to God (or the Cosmos) in terms of a sense of self dignity and self worth.

— Richard Danielpour

Orchestral materials for "Triptych" are available on hire from the publisher:
3.2.2+bcl.3(cbn)/4231/timp.3Perc/pf.hp/str

G. Schirmer/AMP Rental and Performance Department
445 Bellvale Road
Chester, NY 10918
telephone: 845-469-4699
fax: 845-469-7544

Information on Richard Danielpour and his works may be found at www.schirmer.com

Synopsis

When Edward Gaines acquires his deceased brother's Kentucky estate, he pledges to let all the slave families on Maplewood Plantation stay together. However, when he takes a special interest in one of the slaves, Margaret Garner, it is not long before her husband Robert is sent away alone to another plantation. One night, Robert sneaks back to Maplewood and attempts to escape with Margaret and their children to the 'Free State' of Ohio. They are caught and Margaret murders her children in a crime passionel to spare them the indignity of a life of slavery. Margaret is condemned to death and although she is granted clemency at the last minute, she chooses the freedom of the gallows over life as a slave.

Margaret's Lullaby
Act I, scene ii

After a long day of toiling in the fields, the slaves return to their quarters for their evening meal. Margaret, her husband Robert, and Cilla (Robert's mother) are in good spirits as they begin to prepare supper. After grace is said, Margaret insists on seeing her baby. However, Cilla warns her that as a slave Margaret should not become too attached to her child. However, Margaret persists and then settles down to sing a tender lullaby to her daughter.

A Quality Love
Act I, scene iii

Margaret has now been assigned to work in the Maplewood Plantation's main house—the domain of owner Edward Gaines. A large reception is being held to celebrate the marriage of Gaines's daughter Caroline to George Hancock. Naturally, party discussions turn to the nature of love, which then quickly becomes a heated discourse between Gaines and George. The newlyweds break the tension by presenting the traditional "first dance," during which the partygoers join in except Gaines—he is the only person without a partner. Afterwards, he toasts the happy couple. Caroline accidentally rekindles the recent disagreement by asking Margaret for her opinions of love. The local residents haughtily disapprove of Caroline's question and the low social manner in which Gaines appears to run his household, and abruptly depart. Gaines lashes out at his daughter—refusing to be mollified by her, and the newlyweds leave for their honeymoon. Afterwards, as Margaret begins to clear the glasses (while Gaines stays in the background observing her), she takes a moment to reflect on the nature of "a quality love."

Intermezzo
Act II, scene i

The intermezzo is a "moment out of time." Total darkness envelops the stage. Gradually, the image of Margaret, alone, becomes visible. With defiant and noble grandeur, she embraces her life's circumstances.

MARGARET'S LULLABY
from the Opera
MARGARET GARNER
(Act I, Scene 2)

Toni Morrison

Richard Danielpour

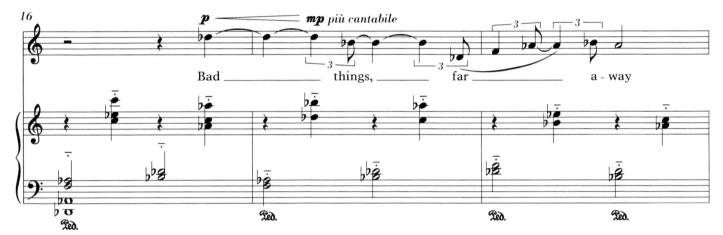

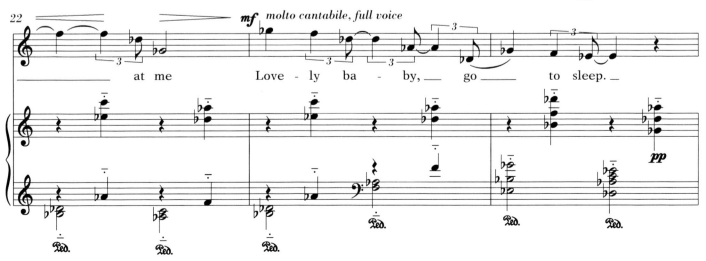

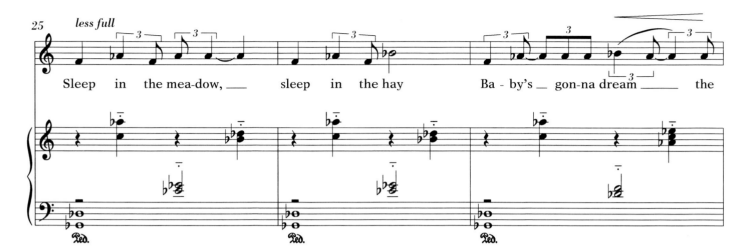

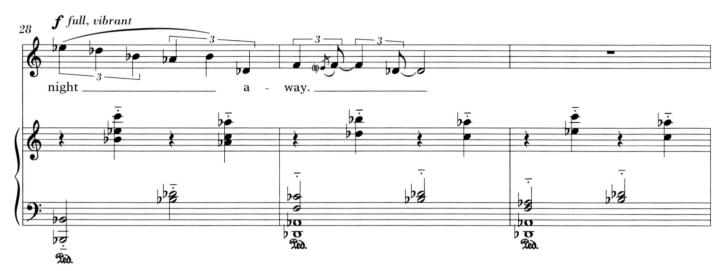

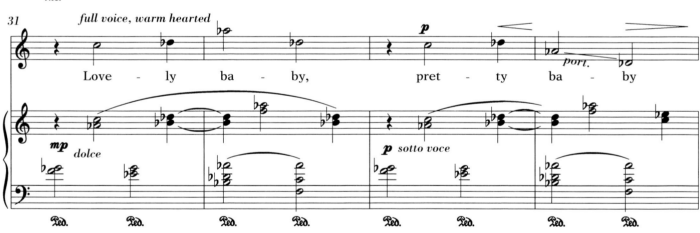

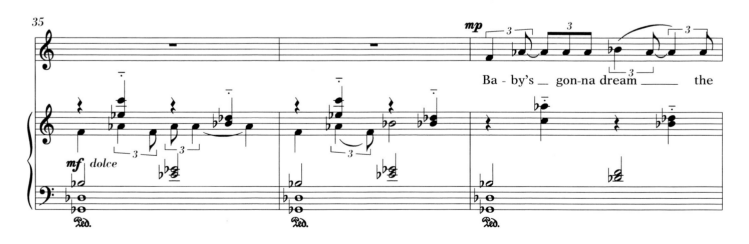

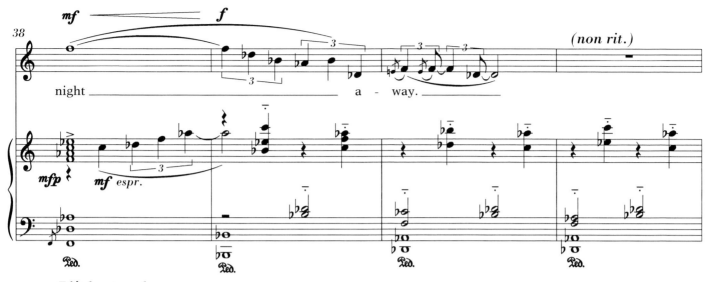

*mm 46–47 ossia: "mmm" (humming)

to Kathleen

A QUALITY LOVE
from the Opera
MARGARET GARNER
(Act I, Scene 3)

Toni Morrison

Richard Danielpour

Intermezzo
from the Opera
MARGARET GARNER

Toni Morrison

Richard Danielpour

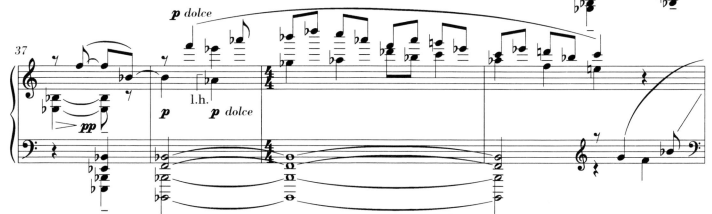

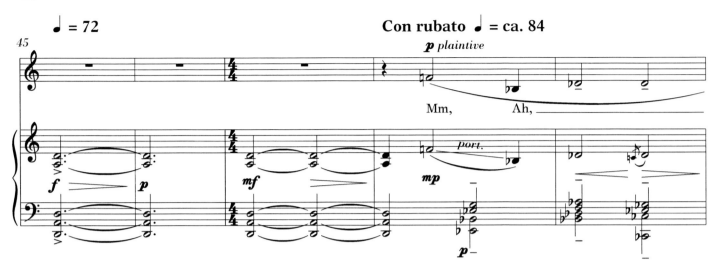

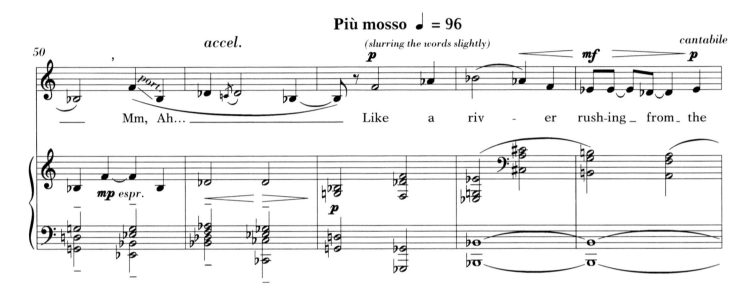

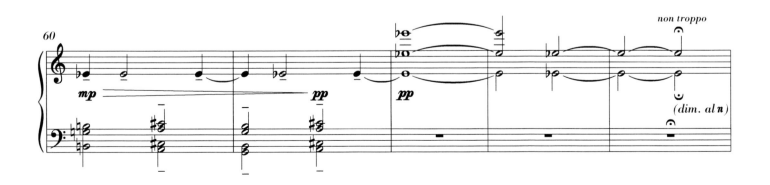

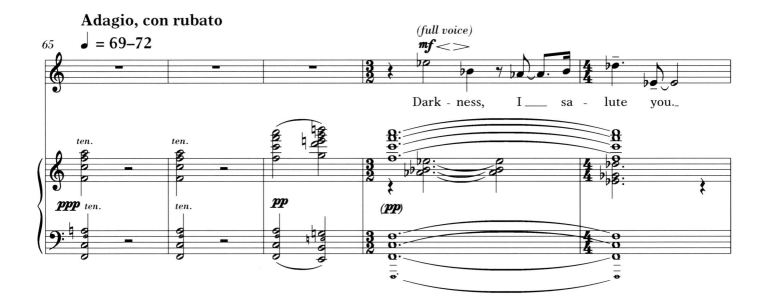

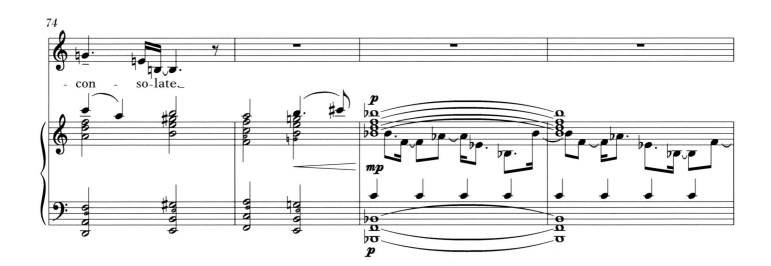

Grief _____ is my plea-sure; _____

thief of life, my lov-er ___ now. _____

Dark - ness, _

_ I ___ sa - lute _____ you. _____